THINK
LIKE A
LAWYER
DON'T
ACT LIKE
ONE

for the three most beautiful girls

THINK LIKE A LAWYER DON'T ACT LIKE ONE

AERNOUD BOURDREZ

© 2009 - 2013 Aernoud Bourdrez

Text and concept: Aernoud Bourdrez
Design and concept: buro van Ons
DTP: Deck vormgeving
Author's photograph: Annique Paalvast

www.thinklikealawyer.info

For questions: aernoud@bourdrezlaw.com

ISBN 978 90 6369 307 7
9th Printing 2016

BIS Publishers
Building Het Sieraad
Postjesweg 1
1057 DT Amsterdam
The Netherlands
www.bispublishers.com
bis@bispublishers.com

Copy this if you dare!

INTRODUCTION

Conflicts are part of life. Usually they're small, but sometimes they blow up into battles that grind your life to a halt. Unfortunately, many conflicts just drag on and on, or worse, escalate. As a lawyer and negotiator, my job is to solve conflicts. Few people know how to avoid or solve a conflict. One person focuses on the issue at hand, but forgets that there's a human being on the other side of the table. Another opts for a friendlier approach, but ends up making too many concessions. And yet another reacts impulsively, lets his ego get involved, worsens the conflict and creates a resentful opponent.

In my practice, I have observed that every conflict – large or small, personal or professional – reveals similar patterns. There are only a few patterns, and they keep resurfacing again and again. In order to solve a conflict, you have to recognize and break through these patterns. In this book I explain how you can do this. There are 75 lessons, not all of which I have come up with myself, but which I have always been able to apply successfully. I show you, for example, that you shouldn't be hard or soft, but both: hard on the problem, but soft on the person. I explain why Freddy Heineken was a good negotiator, how to deal with "cowboys" and hysterical women, why "sorry" is such a great word, and when you should share a bite with someone.

Once you have read this book, you will be able to solve almost any conflict in a simple manner.

Aernoud Bourdrez

CONTENTS

INTRODUCTION

ELEMENTARY RULES

ATTITUDE

TIPS BEFORE YOU BEGIN

APPROACH

BEGIN WITH THE END IN MIND

What is this conflict really about? What actually matters? And what doesn't matter at all? If you feel cheated, it is very likely that you're not seeing straight. You've lost sight of what really matters to you. You're so disappointed, frustrated and furious, that you can only think of one thing: retribution! But getting back at the other person won't make you feel better. And it certainly won't get you what you want. At best, he will lick his wounds for a while. At worst, you'll have a full-blown escalation on your hands. At such times, stop and ask yourself: How do I want to remember this conflict? What will still seem important to me ten years down the road? Will I be proud of the way I handled it? In other words: Begin with the end in mind. ∎

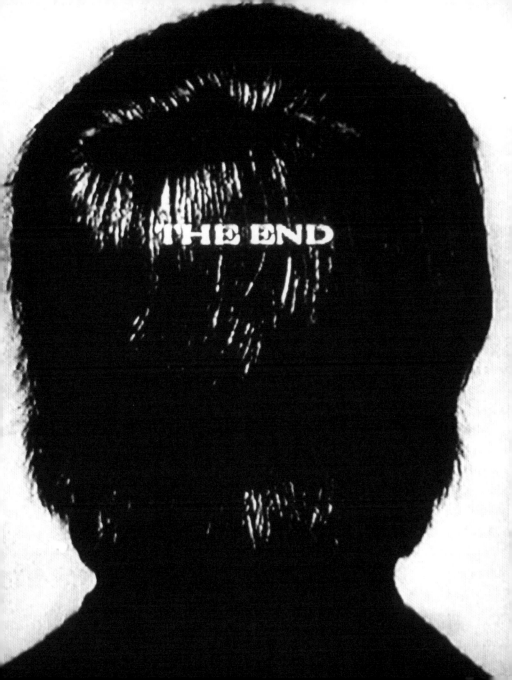

NEVER LOSE SIGHT

A conflict can arise when two people have opposite – thus clashing – interests. That makes it difficult to keep your focus on the goal. Take the Taekwondo fighter in the picture. He's missed out on the bronze medal and he's pissed. You can't really blame him: he's trained his whole life for an Olympic medal. But, in his rage, he kicks the referee in the face. No doubt he's blowing off a lot of steam, but he's also saying goodbye to any chance of an Olympic medal – which, after all, is what he wants. You'll only achieve your objective if you focus on it. ∎

AVOID BICKERING

Let's say a client of yours owes you money. He claims he never got your invoice. You could protest: "That's impossible!" You're not crazy and you know you sent him the bill – over three months ago, as a matter of fact. But then you would be inviting a noisy "Did not! Did so!" discussion. As these – as you might remember from when you were very, very young – lead nowhere. Don't be distracted and remember your objective: to get paid. It is much more effective to remain calm and simply ask him how many days it would take him to pay if you mail him another invoice. This way you'll get a commitment, and a commitment almost always leads to a quick payment. ■

FIGHT FOR YOUR RIGHT

You are what you believe. Fight for what you are. What do you believe in? Creative freedom, respect or money? Then fight for it. Not everyone will agree with you. But everyone will respect you for acting consistently with what you believe. Fight.

THE PURPOSE OF WAR IS PEACE

Imagine that someone violates your rights. Or treats you badly. Or lies to you. You didn't ask for it, but you've got a problem. And there's a big chance that, sooner or later, it will grow into a conflict. To solve the situation you'll have to face it, whether you like it or not. Therefore, don't walk away: make sure you're clear about what your interests are, and then go and discuss the matter to try and resolve it. If this peaceful attempt comes to nothing, then simply take the person to court. Sometimes you have to first strike a blow to reach a solution. ∎

MAN IS NOT BALL

You have a conflict. No need to worry; it happens to the best of us. But play the ball, not the man. True: playing the man can work, but then only one person wins and the relationship is over. Take the Italian soccer player Materazzi. During the 2006 World Cup, a couple of pointed insults he made regarding Zidane's sister made the French star player lose control. He head-butted the Italian and was thrown out of the game. If your objective is to eliminate your opponent, this might work. But if you want to reach an agreement, you'll have to separate your opponent from the problem. Tackle the conflict, not the man. You and he are going to have to seek a solution together. ■

HARD ON THE PROBLEM SOFT ON THE PEOPLE

Mr. Wolf in Pulp Fiction: 'So pretty please, with sugar on top, clean the fuckin' car'

Be hard when it comes to the issue at hand, but be gentle on the person across from you: this may be the most valuable lesson in conflict management. Being hard means that you stand by your principles, by what is essential for you. You don't make any unacceptable concessions. No tampering with market access, artistic freedom, payment obligations, and so on. But be gentle on the person. If you're hard on him, you'll create a conflict - but if you're gentle on the issue, you'll end up regretting the concessions you make. By being hard on the issue and gentle on the person, you'll be successful in your negotiations and gain what there is to be gained. ■

EVOKE EMPATHY

In a room full of babies, if one starts crying, the rest will follow. Nobody escapes empathy. But, as is the case with babies, we feel empathy the strongest when the other is physically present. Therefore, make sure you meet your opponent, in the flesh. Live. Let him see with his own eyes who and what you are: a human, just like him. This increases the chance that he'll empathize with you and your interests. Once this happens, an agreement won't be far off. ■

HAVE
A BITE

Ronald Reagan and Mikhail Gorbachev met for the first time in 1985. Before sitting down, they agreed that they would not be entering into any agreement (yet). This meeting in front of the warm fireplace marked the beginning of the end of the Cold War. Invite the other party for a chat and agree beforehand not to (aim to) enter into an agreement just yet. Have a bite together, or lunch. Just by sitting down and openly exchanging views without any pressure to produce anything has led to countless peace treaties – both big and small. ■

CREATE GOODWILL

A tight contract and a top lawyer might be effective, but goodwill offers you even better protection. If you've got your rival's goodwill, he's less likely to take you for a ride. Goodwill prevents conflicts. Develop goodwill by investing in the personal relationship. No wonder Russians first get drunk together and Finns share a sauna. Friendship first, then down to business.

PATIENTS DON'T SUE DOCTORS THEY LIKE

US insurers investigated which doctors are more likely to be taken to court for their blunders. Their conclusion: the unpleasant ones. Patients don't sue doctors they like. The decisive factor was not related to the doctors' training or the gravity of the error; no, it was the way they treated their patients. By listening well, being reasonable, explaining and, even, frankly admitting mistakes, you too can minimize the chance of a conflict.

DON'T BE THE ONE WHO GETS CHEATED

Even people who have absolutely no respect for anyone's rights at all are selective. They're picky about who they pick on. A lawyer, for instance, is not a favored target; nor is a politician, a police officer or a street fighter. But artists and musicians are popular targets, because they're easy prey. They're generally not good at fighting back. So they are constantly being cheated and robbed. It is a fact that such calculating people exist. Therefore, if there is a risk that you'll be seen as an easy target, make sure you nail down contracts, payment terms and rights. Show that you know your rights. Bring in a lawyer, if only once: show them that you're aware of your rights and your aim to protect them. If you have been to court before, you've got an advantage: you have the aura of someone who has gone all the way. Someone who not only has a weapon, but who isn't afraid to use it. The sharks sense that immediately. Don't be like that small cat, photographed by Ed van der Elsken. He wrote: "Four or five rough and nasty cats rape that cute little cat over and over again. Nevertheless, she seeks it out, the poor little darling." ∎

Serf maar gegrilde en
gemarineerde coquilles
met structuur van
aardpeer; frisse salade
(witlof appel) ...gevulden
... en geschaafde
herfsttruffel   Mag ook
een gebakken ei zijn.

BREAK THE ICE (WITH HUMOR)

When the beer magnate, Freddy Heineken, was kidnapped a number of years ago, the criminals asked him to write down on a piece of paper what he wanted to eat. He wrote the words to the left. It's a list of exquisite food, a gourmet's delight, but it concludes with: "fried eggs are fine too". Heineken's humor broke the ice. His kidnappers started treating him better. Everybody is susceptible to humor. In difficult situations it's one of the best ice breakers. ■

SAY SORRY

That little, five-letter word, "sorry", is priceless. If you really mean it when you say it, you'll clear up more problems than a team of pricey lawyers. ■

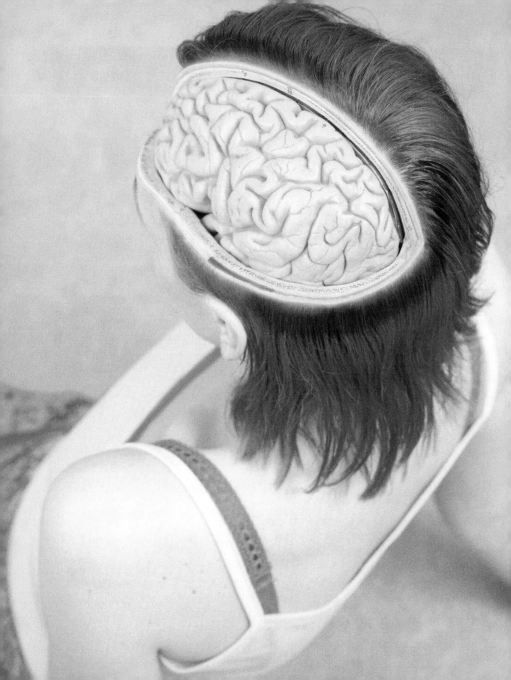

BE CONSCIOUS OF YOUR SUBCONSCIOUS

Many times in a conflict you're not exactly sure what it is that's bugging you. The real reason for the conflict lies buried deep below the surface, in your subconscious. So be conscious of your subconscious. Explore your gut feeling. Retrace what happened – step by step. Find out where that unpleasant feeling comes from. Do you feel unappreciated? Excluded? Humiliated? Are they not taking you seriously? Or do they question your professionalism? By identifying the cause you contain your frustration. This decreases your chances of acting impulsively and further worsening your position. An added advantage: while you're exploring, you're also taking time out for yourself. ■

NEVER ASSUME YOU'RE SMARTER

In 1989, in the semi-finals of the French Open, the world's number one, Ivan Lendl, played Michael Chang, ranked 15th. Lendl only had to get by tiny Chang, and he'd be defending his title in the final against Stefan Edberg. Then the amazing upset happened. Chang beat Lendl. But what was more unbelievable, or hilarious, was how he did it. At game point in the second-last game, Chang hit an underhand serve to the world's top player, and won the game. At match point, Chang befuddled the champion again by standing on the service line to receive serve. Lendl tapped his forehead with his finger indicating what he thought of his opponent's mental state, and promptly served a double fault which lost him the match. You've got to be pretty smart to play stupid. ■

YOUR PERCEPTION IS YOUR REALITY

What does the tiger in this picture perceive: a baby tiger or a piglet? Objective reality doesn't exist – it's all a matter of perception. Each of us walks around with our own version of reality: you do, and so does your opponent. Accept this reality. And then ask yourself whether disputes about the facts are helping to solve your conflict. Are they not? Then move beyond the facts. ■

SEE THE MONKEY INSIDE

How do you handle a conflict with a guy who is extremely unreasonable? He claims he is right, but he's unquestionably wrong. He simply wants to win, to triumph. Typical alpha-male behavior. Many would react by trying to justify his conduct. However, there is no justification. But there is an explanation. Primatologist Frans de Waal has written a lot about what drives chimps, our close primate cousins. The alpha male is driven mostly by domination. Of course, he also wants the perks that come with being the boss: the tastiest food and most attractive females. So, forget justification. Just identify your opponent's alpha-male driver, and you have the key to solving your conflict. ∎

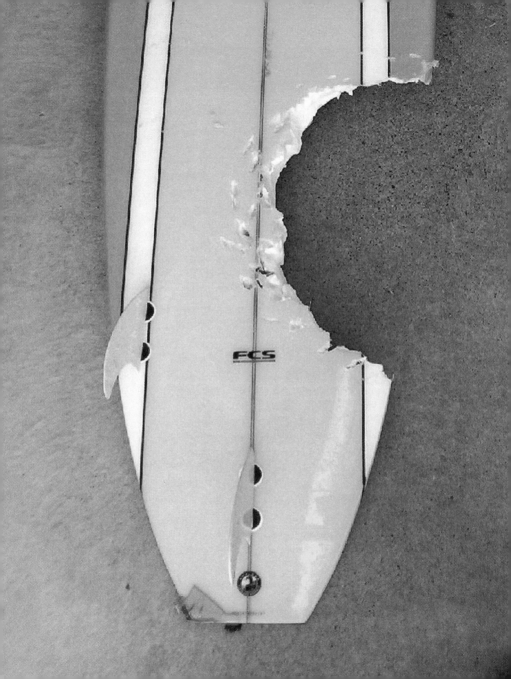

DON'T TAKE IT PERSONALLY

You're facing a selfish boss, creditor or a annoying client. And he is not being very nice. In fact, he's letting you have it: insidious insinuations, low blows and downright insults. Don't take it personally. Stay cool. Think of yourself as the representative of your own virtual limited liability company: "Me, myself and I, Inc." All those words will flow of you, like water off a duck's back. ∎

LOSE YOUR PATIENCE, LOSE THE GAME

The highest trump card in conflict situations is the ace of patience. The more patience you have, the stronger your position. ∎

21

KNOW YOUR ENEMY

If you know the enemy and know yourself
you need not fear the results of a hundred battles.
(The Art of War, Sun Tzu, sixth-century Chinese general and philosopher)

Knowledge is power – especially at the negotiating table. So make sure you know all there is to know. Before you start, lay out all the details and circumstances that led to the conflict. Immerse yourself in your opponent: What kind of person is he? What are his weaknesses? Where do his vulnerabilities lie? Is he vain? What's he scared of? What gets him excited? Why is he fighting you? What does he want? And then address these same questions regarding yourself. You have to know yourself too. Sounds pretty obvious, but very few actually do this. Know yourself, know the enemy and know the facts – through and through. Because a poorly prepared case is a lost case. ■

 # 22

UNDER-PROMISE, OVER-DELIVER

Creating great expectations is tempting, but not always wise. If you end up delivering less than you promised, you make a conflict more likely to occur. Promise less than you'll deliver and you'll have a satisfied client. ∎

 # 23

KNOW WHAT YOU'RE NOT GOING TO SAY

Knowing what you're going to say: useful.
Knowing what you're not going to say: crucial.
Saying what you shouldn't have said: fatal.

IF YOU BARK, BITE TOO

Don't go soft if someone misses a deadline. Do what you said you would do: Bite! The next deadline will be taken a lot more seriously. ■

PICK YOUR ENEMY

The former mayor of Rotterdam, Bram Peper, caused a scandal when he submitted an expense claim for tens of thousands of euros to his employer, the City of Rotterdam. Allegedly, he had spent the money on private trips and fancy dinners. Peper played it well. He counterattacked and targeted the most attractive opponent – that is, the opponent whose defeat would benefit him most. He picked KPMG, the accountants. They had acted wrongfully: they had gone public with the details of their report. He started legal action against them, they settled for an enormous amount, and his name was cleared in the media. ■

26

KNOW YOUR BATNA

You're in a conflict and you're about to negotiate. Think of your alternatives if a settlement is not reached. In other terms, know your BATNA, or your Best Alternative To a Negotiated Agreement. What will happen if you end up in court? If your case is strong, then you can aim high. If it's weak, chances are you'll leave the court room empty handed. Here's how to improve your BATNA: Build a solid case file. Hire a good lawyer. Subtly let your opponent know that you have the means and the patience to use the file and the lawyer. The Chinese owner of the house in this picture knows all about this. ∎

27 KISS

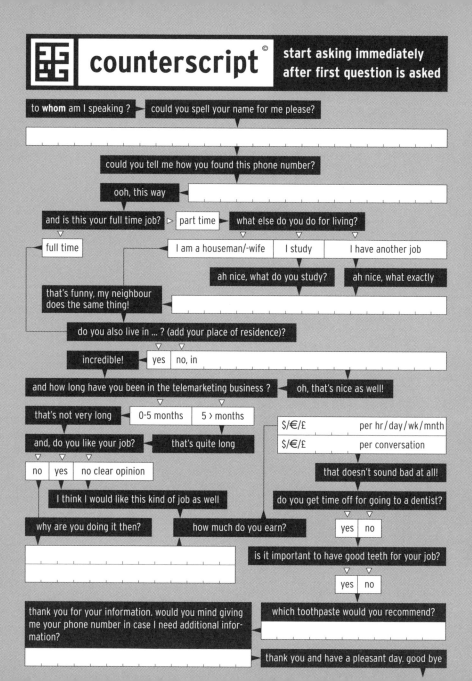

COUNTER WITH A QUESTION

If you've been maneuvered into an awkward spot: start asking questions. Lots of them. You'll regain control of the situation. Dutch artist Martijn Engelbregt applied this principle quite nicely in his "counterscript". Here's the idea: say you're being bugged by a telephone polltaker. Don't answer his questions, ask questions of your own. This way, you'll buy time and control the direction in which the dialogue moves. By asking questions you get the upper hand. ■

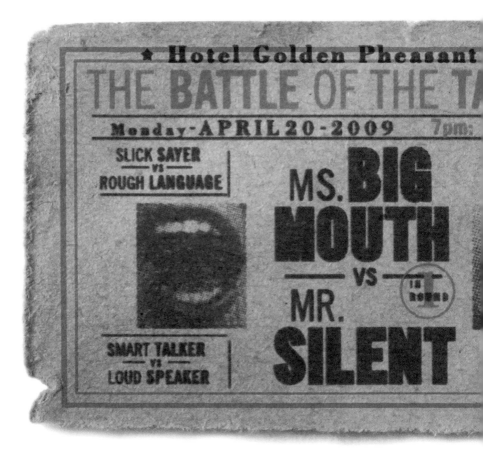

★ Hotel Golden Pheasant

THE **BATTLE** OF THE TA

Monday · APRIL 20 · 2009   7pm:

SLICK SAYER
— vs —
ROUGH LANGUAGE

SMART TALKER
— vs —
LOUD SPEAKER

MS. **BIG MOUTH**
— vs —
MR. **SILENT**

1st ROUND

29

USE THE POWER OF SILENCE

Silence is a powerful negotiating weapon. Listen more than you speak, and let the silences be. Your adversary, out of embarrassment or discomfort, will fill in the gaps. He'll talk away and probably say things he doesn't want to say. Moreover, what you don't say can't be held against you. ∎

30

PACE YOURSELF

Towards the end of the 1959 US Grand Prix, racing driver Jack Brabham was in the lead and sitting pretty. The race was won ...virtually. But just before the finish line his engine sputtered and then stopped: the tank was empty. Brabham had stepped on the gas too much and had run out. In desperation, he started pushing his car to the finish line, but was overtaken just before getting there. Don't make the same mistake as Brabham (and many negotiators). Remember that the finish line is very far down the road and pace yourself: spread your energies along the whole course. ∎

31

TAKE ONE STEP AT A TIME

Solutions take time. They involve many steps. First you have to lay out the problem. Then negotiate. Then put the agreement down on paper. And then you have to make sure it is complied with. If not, then you have to take follow-up steps. The point is that you have to concentrate on the step in question. It makes sense, because if you're too concerned about steps later down the line, you're likely to stumble. ■

'NEVER NEVER NEVER GIVE IN'

Sir Winston Churchill, speech to Harrow School students (1941)

DEUTSCHER
FUSSBALL-BUND

KNVB

STAY SHARP UNTIL THE BITTER END

A victor is someone who wins the last battle. Fight to the end. German soccer players are masters at this – they call it *Kampfkraft*, or combat strength. One could say that their national team, the Mannschaft, holds the patent for Kampfkraft. Gyuri "professor penalty" Vergouw has conducted extensive research into this. His work confirms the Teutonic reputation for battling persistence: Germans score significantly more in the last minute of play than any other team. If you're in the last stage of your conflict, brace yourself once more and stay mad and focused. Don't run the risk of having your victory slip through your fingers at the very last moment. Such defeats are the most painful of all. ■

34

FILE
A CLAIM

Suppose someone steals your brilliant idea for a TV programme. He works it into a format, and then tries to sell it to a producer or broadcaster. In such a case, it makes a lot of sense to file a claim – a paralyzing claim. Your lawyer writes the thief a letter making the claim and demanding damages. That will do it. The format is dead: no buyer will risk burning his fingers on a product with a claim attached. ∎

35

'SOMETIMES THE SECOND-BEST OPTION LEADS TO THE BEST RESULT'

(Bobby Fischer 1943 – 2008, Chess Grandmaster)

■

36

WALK AWAY FOR A CHANGE

Sometimes, walking out of a negotiation – however difficult – is the only way of getting what you want. If the opponent fears a good result is getting away from him, then he'll be more disposed to make concessions. ∎

COUNT
TO
TEN

People from all over the world fly to Harvard University to participate in its renowned Program on Negotiation. One of the main lessons they take home is: "Count to ten". ∎

FIND THE WEAK SPOT

Dynamite Show, 31 December 2005, Tokyo

Heath Herring and Yoshihiro Nakao engage in a stare-off in the free-fighting ring on New Year's eve: it's the pre-fight, forehead-to-forehead, staring contest. All of a sudden, Nakao kisses Herring on the mouth. Herring is not amused. He gives Nakao a powerful right hook. Nakao falls to the mat and can't get up – at least that's what it looks like. Herring is furious. He knows what's coming. After all, he's just floored his opponent before the starting bell. "He kissed me on the lips like a homosexual!" he shouts. "I'm not gay!" Herring is disqualified. Nakao wins without landing a single blow – but with a well-placed kiss. Yoshihiro "Kiss" Nakao found Herring's weakest spot. ∎

39

DELEGATE THE PROBLEM

Sam's lying in bed, but can't sleep. Sarah asks him what's wrong. "Tomorrow I have to pay Max 5,000 euros, but I don't have it." "Is that it?" says Sarah. She picks up the phone and calls Max. "Hi Max," she says. "Listen, Sam was supposed to pay you tomorrow, but he doesn't have the money. Bye!" and hangs up. "Now you can sleep and Max can't." ■

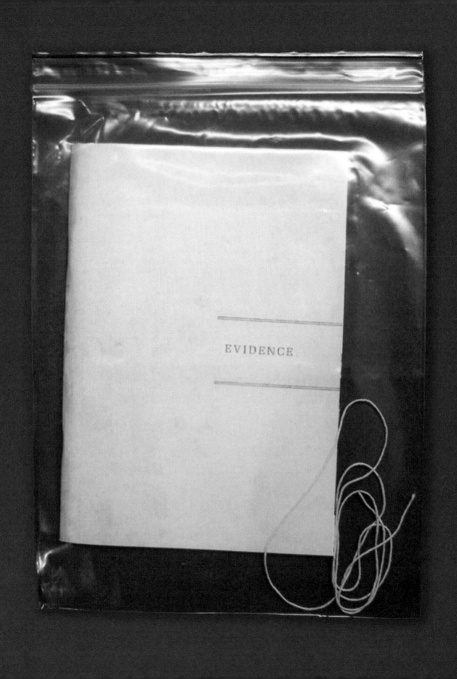

CONFIRM AGREEMENTS

Agreements in black and white are most likely to be observed. It's logical: a written agreement is evidence. E-mails are perfect for this, but the tone is important. You can write: "I hereby confirm that the photographic material that is subject to our agreement cannot be used outside of the United States without the payment of extra compensation." But this could be taken as a sign that you don't trust them. Why not write: "I look back on our fruitful meeting with pleasure. If you would also like to use my pictures outside of the US, I would be pleased to send you an offer for such use." This keeps the relationship friendly and implies that you are willing to grant further rights. But most importantly, you have clearly implied – in document form – that they only have the rights for the United States, and that if they use the photos elsewhere, they are obligated to pay you extra for this. Confirm agreements using e-mail, and build up a case file. ∎

41

SIT SIDE BY SIDE

Say, you're diametrically opposed to someone in a conflict. Then you will only aggravate the tension if you, literally, sit diametrically opposite each other at the negotiating table. That's why mediators prefer round tables. If you want to reach an agreement, it helps to change your physical position with regard to your opponent. For change, try sitting next to him. It also helps to be on the same side more abstractly: focus on a common goal together – or talk about a common enemy. Make sure you're both facing the same direction, shoulder to shoulder. Accentuate what you have in common, not what divides you. ■

42

KEEP THE HUMAN FACTOR IN MIND

Never underestimate the human factor. If the other person doesn't like your face, he'll do everything to prevent an outcome that benefits you. Be aware of this basic truth. Do your best to ensure that the person likes you, or is favorably disposed to you, as a person. Then you'll often get more than you're entitled to – and a pleasant experience into the bargain. ■

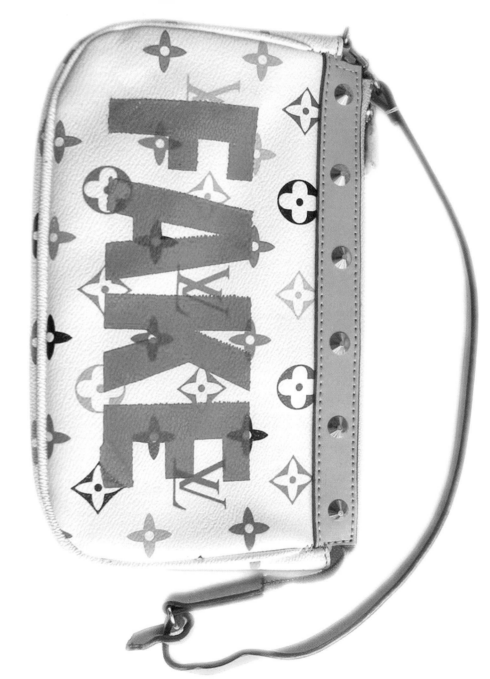

CALL A SPADE A SPADE

Parties in a conflict often beat around the bush. So long as a spade is not called a spade, their attempts to reach a solution get them no-where. Say what everybody is thinking, but doesn't dare to say. You'll clear the air and get your agreement faster. ■

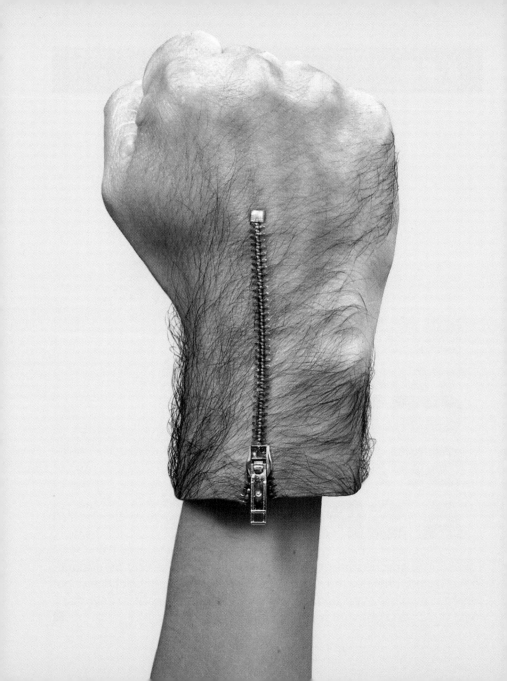

44

SOMETIMES, BANG THE TABLE

An art collector invites you to his home for dinner. Reproductions of Monet's paintings of flowers and Degas' dancers decorate the walls. Nice, but ... a little boring. You go to the bathroom and, there, next to the window, hangs a very racy work by Jeff Koons. Your perception of your new friend 's collection changes radically. He likes Monet not because he has no guts, but because of aesthetic conviction – and he also likes Koons. Apply this lesson to your negotiations. If you opt for a nice, friendly approach, make sure that your opponent knows you're just as capable of banging your fist on the table if he pushes you far enough. Let him know that your friendliness is a reflection of choice, conviction, and not of weakness. Show that you're no stranger to a tough stance.

■

"FORTY EUROS?! AND WHEN WILL YOU HAVE IT READY?!"

45

DO
THE
UNEXPECTED

Your light is broken and you're stopped by an officer. You try to per-
suade him that what you did wasn't that wrong. By saying this, you're
actually telling him that he is wrong. But he's familiar with that reaction. He encounters it a hundred times a week. So he tells you that he
can see perfectly well what you're doing and that the fine is justified.
He has no choice. Behave unexpectedly. Catch him off-guard. Distract
him. You've now opened the door to a no-ticket solution. If someone
has decided to give you a hard time, your unexpected response can
work miracles. ■

 # 46

BE PREPARED TO DO IT

Many who are party to a conflict – particularly large companies – deal with conflict situations by dragging their feet. That's not so stupid. A delaying strategy often works: many cases just die a slow death and disappear. If your opponent does this, you might have to get rough: you don't have to like it, but you have to be prepared to do it. And you've got to let them know. The moment you hear that sound of dragging feet, take legal action or call in the media. They'll listen, and they'll often want to settle fast. As Al Capone once said: "You can get much further with a kind word and a gun than you can with a kind word alone." ■

OFFER A GRACEFUL EXIT

You're in the middle of a conflict and your opposite party makes a blunder, an obvious mistake. Resist the temptation to take immediate advantage of it. Turn a blind eye to it, but subtly let him know that you're intentionally turning a blind eye to it. This way, he won't be (completely) embarrassed and you speed up the resolution of the conflict. Offer the other party a graceful exit and he will owe you. One consequence of this is that he'll be well disposed to reaching a result that will please you too. ■

☐ YOU ARE WITH US OR

☐ YOU ARE AGAINST US

Gorilla

SNIFF OUT THE FALLACY

Before he invaded Iraq, George W. Bush announced to the world: "You're either with us or you're against us." A third option – remaining neutral – he chose not to mention. A fallacy. A fallacy is a form of reasoning that seems reasonable, but isn't. What's hard about a fallacy is that you often sense that there's something wrong with the logic, but you can't put your finger on it. Always ask yourself: What is the guy's faulty assumption? Sniff out the fallacy. ∎

#49

BEWARE
OF
THE
CATCH

"If you let me crack three eggs on your head, I'll give you 25 euros."
An interesting offer, and one that quite a few younger brothers jumped
at: 25 euros! After the second egg, the elder brother declares that he
isn't going to crack the third one after all: no 25 euros then. Shrewd
negotiators use this kind of tactic too. They connect payment to conditions over which you have no control at all. One phrase captures this
trickery: Do not accept those conditions! ∎

JOHN J. RAMBO

IT STARTED WHEN HE HIT BACK

Every day, people infringe the rights and legitimate interests of others. And every day the guilty parties scream blue murder when accused – as if the victims caused the problem. If your rights and interests are trampled on, then you're quite right to do something about it. Don't be thrown off by a cry of indignation. Or as Rambo put it: "They drew first blood."

■

STICK TO YOUR PRINCIPLES

Sir Winston Churchill turns to the woman sitting next to him at a dinner: "Would you sleep with me for a million pounds?" "Well… I suppose so," she responds. "All right." says Churchill. "Would you sleep with me for ten pounds?" "Of course not! What kind of woman do you think I am?" she exclaims. "Madam, we've already established that you are a whore, we are now haggling over the price." Stick to your principles. Don't abandon them at any price. If you do, it will be used against you, for sure. ∎

The reader, hereinafter referred to as the "unaware", is assumed to have read and accepted the conditions that follow hereafter. The unaware waives his rights to file any claim against the author, hereinafter referred to as the "inviolable", or of any third party, including designers, desk-top publishers, printers and publishers, that the inviolable may involve in the production of this book, based on any alleged shortcomings, such as but not limited to any claim that the lessons should be universally applicable, or any shortcoming in the fact that these lessons do not immediately or completely cause the effect that the unaware had expected them to have and, according to him, ought to have been expected to have. Without prejudice to the principle that every person should know the law, the unaware declares to have knowledge of the intellectual property and other rights of the inviolable, the publisher and those third parties assigned by the inviolable, and furthermore with the rights of the inviolable to, both in the Netherlands and the Netherlands, act against every form of infringement of these rights. The unaware hereby also waives his rights to appeal against the disclaimer, which reads "Copy if you dare". The unaware is fully aware that this sentence is not an invitation, nor can it be understood to be an invitation or a form of approbation to violate the rights of the inviolable, the publisher or any other third party that might be involved. This minuscule print has been consciously maintained minuscule to prevent the unaware from being alarmed by the number of pages that is necessary to describe the wide variety of applicable conditions that can or could cause the inviolable, the publisher or possible involved third parties, harm. Minuscule letters are, as a rule, purposefully formulated in a complicated manner, with a view to minimizing the chances of the unaware being informed, which also minimizes the chance of a possible claim aimed at the inviolable. Because the unaware, in general, is not informed of the precise content of the small print, he remains ignorant and vulnerable in the event the inviolable is in default, as well as unaware of important information which in the legal procedure can be used against the unaware. It can be the case that the unaware misses out on attractive possibilities, such as the undertaking made herein by the inviolable to make the unaware eligible for a dinner for two at Chinese Restaurant Libelle in Heerhugowaard, the Netherlands, or any other Chinese Restaurant in the world (with a maximum of two hundred and fifty euros), if the unaware is the first to send an e-mail to bourdrez@use-ip.com making an official request and containing the words "me me me" in the subject. In order to prevent the inviolable and the publisher's being placed in an undesirable position, the aforementioned e-mail must be sent prior to the fifteenth day of August of the year two-thousand and thirteen. The reader, hereinafter referred to as the "unaware", is assumed to have read and accepted the conditions that follow hereafter. The unaware waives his rights to file any claim against the author, hereinafter referred to as the "inviolable", or of any third party, including designers, desk-top publishers, printers and publishers, that the inviolable may involve in the production of this book, based on any alleged shortcomings, such as but not limited to any claim that the lessons should be universally applicable, or any shortcoming in the fact that these lessons do not immediately or completely cause the effect that the unaware had expected them to have and, according to him, ought to have been expected to have. Without prejudice to the principle that every person should know the law, the unaware declares to have knowledge of the intellectual property and other rights of the inviolable, the publisher and those third parties assigned by the inviolable, and furthermore with the rights of the inviolable to, both in the Netherlands and the Netherlands, act against every form of infringement of these rights. The unaware hereby also waives his rights to appeal against the disclaimer, which reads "Copy if you dare". The unaware is fully aware that this sentence is not an invitation, nor can it be understood to be an invitation or a form of approbation to violate the rights of the inviolable, the publisher or any other third party that might be involved. This minuscule print has been consciously maintained minuscule to prevent the unaware from being alarmed by the number of pages that is necessary to describe the wide variety of applicable conditions that can or could cause the inviolable, the publisher or possible involved third parties, harm. Minuscule letters are, as a rule, purposefully formulated in a complicated manner, with a view to minimizing the chances of the unaware being informed, which minimizes the chance of a possible claim aimed at the inviolable. Because the unaware, in general, is not informed of the precise content of the small print, he remains ignorant and vulnerable in the event the inviolable is in default, as well as unaware of important information which in the legal procedure can be used against the unaware. It can be the case that the unaware misses out on attractive possibilities, such as the undertaking made herein by the inviolable to make the unaware eligible for a dinner for two at Chinese Restaurant Libelle in Heerhugowaard, the Netherlands, or any other Chinese Restaurant in the world (with a maximum of two hundred and fifty euros), if the unaware is the first to send an e-mail to bourdrez@use-ip.com making an official request and containing the words "me me me" in the subject. In order to prevent the inviolable and the publisher's being placed in an undesirable position, the aforementioned e-mail must be sent prior to the fifteenth day of August of the year two-thousand and thirteen. The reader, hereinafter referred to as the "unaware", is assumed to have read and accepted the conditions that follow hereafter. The unaware waives his rights to file any claim against the author, hereinafter referred to as the "inviolable", or of any third party, including designers, desk-top publishers, printers and publishers, that the inviolable may involve in the production of this book, based on any alleged shortcomings, such as but not limited to any claim that the lessons should be universally applicable, or any shortcoming in the fact that these lessons do not immediately or completely cause the effect that the unaware had expected them to have and, according to him, ought to have been expected to have. Without prejudice to the principle that every person should know the law, the unaware declares to have knowledge of the intellectual property and other rights of the inviolable, the publisher and those third parties assigned by the inviolable, and furthermore with the rights of the inviolable to, both in the Netherlands and the Netherlands, act against every form of infringement of these rights. The unaware hereby also waives his rights to appeal against the disclaimer, which reads "Copy if you dare". The unaware is fully aware that this sentence is not an invitation, nor can it be understood to be an invitation or a form of approbation to violate the rights of the inviolable, the publisher or any other third party that might be involved. This minuscule print has been consciously maintained minuscule to prevent the unaware from being alarmed by the number of pages that is necessary to describe the wide variety of applicable conditions that can or could cause the inviolable, the publisher or possible involved third parties, harm. Minuscule letters are, as a rule, purposefully formulated in a complicated manner, with a view to minimizing the chances of the unaware being informed, which also minimizes the chance of a possible claim aimed at the inviolable. Because the unaware, in general, is not informed of the precise content of the small print, he remains ignorant and vulnerable in the event the inviolable is in default, as well as unaware of important information which in the legal procedure can be used against the unaware. It can be the case that the unaware misses out on attractive possibilities, such as the undertaking made herein by the inviolable to make the unaware eligible for a dinner for two at Chinese Restaurant Libelle in Heerhugowaard, the Netherlands, or any other Chinese Restaurant in the world (with a maximum of two hundred and fifty euros), if the unaware is the first to send an e-mail to bourdrez@use-ip.com making an official request and containing the words "me me me" in the subject. In order to prevent the inviolable and the publisher's being placed in an undesirable position, the aforementioned e-mail must be sent prior to the fifteenth day of August of the year two-thousand and thirteen.

BEWARE OF GOODWILL KILLERS

Too many words, too many letters, opaque language, endless general conditions, penalty clauses, and impossibly tiny print are all goodwill killers. Contracts of this sort can actually divide the parties. Indeed, experience teaches us that such dense, entangled, labyrinthine documents destroy the trust that is so crucial for collaborations. Always ask yourself whether you can avoid these killers. ■

53

AVOID SPOILSPORTS

Lawyers can be real spoilsports. They tend to seek safety, they're worrywarts: they see pitfalls everywhere. They even see them on the road. What they don't see is that one simply drives by the vast majority of pitfalls – without seeing or being seen by them. It also happens that a lawyer might be more interested in showing his intellect and professional competence than in getting a breakthrough in your case. This doesn't help you much. So, when you hire a lawyer, make sure you've got the kind of lawyer you need. If you get one who focuses only on the legal case, and ignores the person you're having a dispute with, then there is a good chance that the conflict will escalate. A spoilsport can spoil your chances of a good outcome. ∎

54

INSIST ON QUID PRO QUO

Why on earth would you give something away, just like that, with nothing in return? Hardened negotiators will always try to get you to. After the agreement has been reached, they'll ask you casually whether they could have the copyrights as well. Or half-way through the process, they send you a contract with a clause stating that you cannot work for a competitor of theirs ever again. Hand over your rights, hand over your freedom, just like that? Don't do it, ever. Remember: quid pro quo.

55

DON'T LOSE OUT TWICE

It happens a lot: in the middle of a job, your client transfers the job to someone else. To someone who charges less, for example. You can climb onto your high horse and send him a severe letter demanding full compensation. But now that you know that money is what drives him, you also know that it's unlikely that he'll bend on this. If you know in advance that you will (probably) not get your money, ask yourself whether a demand is the most effective course of action. Naturally, you shouldn't accept a loss just like that. But often there are other ways of being compensated: with a new assignment, for instance. ■

56

FALSIFY!

If you believe your opponent is an immoral scoundrel, then you'll go looking for hard evidence to prove it. You want to convince yourself and the outside world that you're right. And he who seeks shall find. This happens a lot – it's called confirmation bias. Do you do this? Well, stop doing it. Try to find evidence to the contrary, for evidence that you are wrong. Not easy, but possible – and very inspiring. Chances are you'll discover another angle from which to approach your conflict, which will lead you closer to a solution. ∎

Gorilla

57

IF IT DOESN'T WORK, DO IT DIFFERENTLY

One day, a photographer was surprised to see one of his pictures in a folder of a big international bank. He contacted them. At first, the bank disputed his copyright. Then they disputed the infringement. Then they disputed the amount of damages. And so on: after every concession, they stood and fought again. And the photographer politely followed each of their absurd retreats and defeated them at every new position. But he essentially got nowhere: for all his battling, he wasn't getting his damage compensation. If your opponent keeps coming up with new objections, don't play his game. Take a different approach: roll out the big guns. Hire a lawyer or seek media publicity. ■

58

AVOID DOUBLE DIRT

"Double dirt" is a term used in Dutch detergent ads to indicate how soiled something is. Not just dirty, but twice as dirty, filthy. People in the creative industry are particularly victimized by double-dirt attacks to their rights. The attackers first commit the infringement, then they challenge the illegality of what they've done, and then they resort to lying about the extent of the infringement. Take a distant attitude from this kind of situation, calmly take note of every layer of dirt. When confronting the other person, don't focus on one layer alone, but thrust the whole pile of filth under his nose. There's a very good chance he'll back down. ■

59

BEWARE
OF
OPEN
ENDINGS

Reach a clear agreement about who does what, and when. Don't accept a "We'll give you a call." ∎

REFUSE UNDER-PAYMENT

People who feel they are not paid enough won't work as happily – or as well – as those who feel they're being justly compensated. Payment is a form of appreciation, a measure of respect. Your client might feel selfsatisfied when paying you less than you're worth, but he will pay extra in the form of resentment and a possible conflict. Make sure you're paid what you're worth. ■

61

DEFINE YOUR MINIMUM DEMANDS

I want this man DEAD!
I want his family DEAD!
I want his house burnt to the ground.
I wanna go there in the middle of the night and
I wanna piss on his ashes!
(Al Capone, 1899 – 1947)

Be like Al Capone: make your minimum demands amply clear. It avoids misunderstandings. ∎

REFER TO CLONE CASES

Stella Liebeck of Albuquerque, New Mexico, scalded her private parts when she drove away too fast from a McDonald's restaurant with a hot cup of coffee on her lap. McDonald's was aware that its coffee was too hot: it had already received a number of complaints. But it hadn't done anything about it, due to cost reasons. Reason enough for a jury to grant Ms. Liebeck damages of 2.7 million dollars. However absurd the amount might seem, it wasn't remarkable. Her lawyer referred extensively to comparable cases that led to such damages. And that did it. This principle applies to every negotiating situation. Back up the fees you charge with objective criteria, refer to comparable situations. The ball is then in the other person's court to justify why he should pay you less. And that's often pretty tough. ■

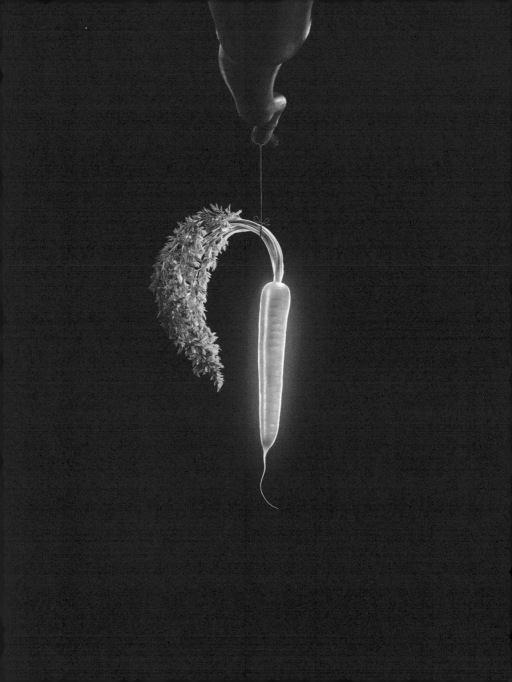

SWEETEN THE DEAL, SWEETEN THE OTHER

Offer something that doesn't cost you much, but that the other person values greatly. This gives him a stimulus to agree with your proposal. If the conflict is about the amount needed to settle an agreement, he might agree to pay more if he can pay in installments. If you're not in a rush, it makes no difference to you – and you get your money in the end. Make it in his interest to work toward a solution. ■

when would you like to pay?

 # 64

GIVE
THEM
A SAY

"When would you like to pay?" That seems a strange question to ask someone who should have paid you long before. But by giving the other party a say in setting the new deadline for him to meet his obligation, you draw him into the decision-making. And paying before a self-defined deadline always hurts a little less. If you give him an extra week beyond that, then the chance that he'll pay becomes even greater. And, of course, don't forget to confirm all this by e-mail. ■

IT'S NOT ABOUT THE DOG

Dr. Phil resolves a marital conflict in one of his TV shows. The issue is the couple's dog. From her point of view, the pet costs too much and his farts stink. From the husband's point of view, what she says is nonsense: she's just bitching again. This gets her even angrier. Enter Dr. Phil with the show's message: "It's not about the dog!" The real problem is that the woman feels neglected. When her husband comes home in the evening, the first thing he does is give the dog a long-drawn-out cuddle, he then briefly greets his wife. Always look for the story behind the story. You'll only solve the problem, if you know what the real problem is. ∎

LOOK BEYOND WORDS

"I have a warm spot in my heart for animals."
(Prince Bernard, founder of the World Wildlife Fund)

Only 7% of your message is expressed in your words. The other 93% is in your intonation, gestures, facial expression, demeanor, clothes, hairstyle, or the gun leaning against your shoulder. Your behavior and body language are far more expressive than what you say. And no word you utter can neutralize what you show or what your body communicates. Keep that in mind. ■

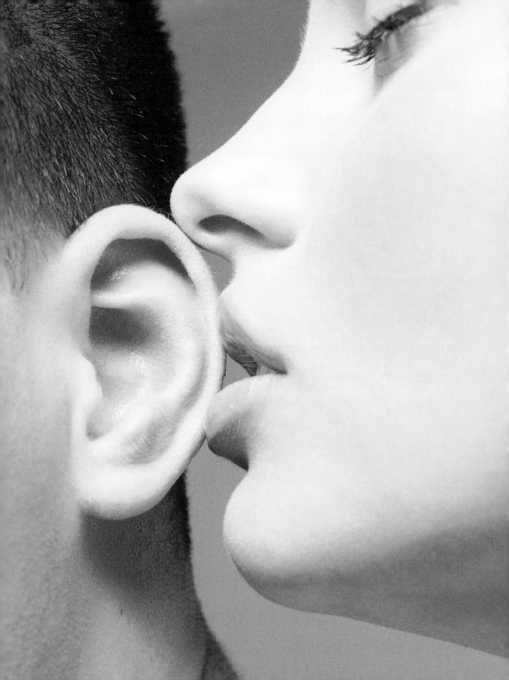

67

TOUCH HIM

Scientists at the University of Minnesota conducted two experiments. In the first, one of the researchers left a coin in a telephone booth and then hid nearby. When he saw that someone had found his coin, he walked up to them and asked: "Did you happen to find my coin?" One quarter of the people gave him back his coin. In the second experiment, the set-up was the same, except that the researcher first touched the elbow of the people before asking them whether they had found his coin. As many as three-quarters of these participants returned the coin. A slight physical touch establishes a bond – and a bond does wonders for negotiations. ■

68

FORM VS. CONTENT

If you're in a conflict and you want to make something perfectly clear, then the manner in which you do it – the form you use – is essential. The wrong form will transmit the wrong message. You lose. Mumbling, delays, typos, unreadable letters, bad grammar, mistaken references to facts, using smileys or microscopic fonts: they can be grounds for not taking you seriously or even for dismissing you. A nice example is illustrated by this photograph. It's of Ms. Verdonk, the Dutch politician. She's standing on a briefcase to give the impression that she's taller than she really is (not the first politician to have a height complex). Whatever Ms. Verdonk may say, she certainly won't be given the benefit of the doubt. ∎

69

AGREE TO DISAGREE

When you're negotiating in a conflict it's easy to slip into "did not, did so" arguments about things that are completely irrelevant. This is obviously counter-productive: it reinforces differences, while your goal is precisely the opposite. Declare out loud that you think it's fine to agree to disagree on side issues. Once that's done, you can focus on the central issue, which is why you came to the table in the first place. ∎

70

KNOW YOUR EGO

Your ego is your self-image. But it's an image that often clashes with reality. Egos often get in the way of negotiations. Does your self- image say you're intelligent? Or the prince of negotiators? Or that you're always right (except when you think you're wrong)? Then you have a problem if these qualities are not confirmed – or actually disproved – in the real world, around the negotiations table. Your reaction will then be to try to rescue your ego. But the conflict has nothing to do with your ego. Deal with it when you get home. Take a good look at your ego. Get it to fit reality. And if this isn't possible, make sure your ego doesn't obstruct your path to an agreement. ■

71

BEWARE OF COWBOYS

"What do you mean?! I never borrowed that gun. Anyhow, I gave it back to you. And, also, the thing was already broken when you lent it to me!" Someone who talks like this is a "cowboy". Cowboys use the most puzzling arguments. They are not very impressed by a summons or a writ, and they don't take agreements too seriously. Even if your legal case is strong, if your opponent is a cowboy it can be very difficult to get any justice. Ask yourself whether he's a cowboy. If he is, then pull out some heavier artillery. ■

HYSTERICAL PAROXYSM

A WONDERFUL HEALER STATES
HERE IS HEALTH
THROUGH **THE MAGIC POWER** OF
FINE GENTLE
MASSAGE

72

SPOT THE HYSTERICAL PERSON

Sometimes your opponent is a hysteric. These characters try to win their battles by employing a torrent of unconnected and irrelevant arguments, one more absurd than the other. The arguments are sometimes so offensive that it will be tempting to respond to each and every insult. But that makes no sense: he'll simply launch another barrage at you. Once a hysteric, always a hysteric.

Up until the beginning of the last century, people thought that only women suffered from hysterias, and the way to cure them was to masturbate them. Since the treatment was labour-intensive for the doctor, the vibrator was invented. Today, there are simpler ways of fighting hysteria. Cut the hysteric's torrent: deal with the two most absurd arguments, and in order to avoid that the hysteric assumes that you agree with the others, conclude with the comment that countering all of his arguments would be going too far. ∎

LIE CAREFULLY

Neurologist Alan Hirsch and psychiatrist Charles Wolf discovered that when someone lies, certain chemicals are released in the body which cause the mucous membrane in the nose to swell. At the same time, the blood pressure increases, so that the extremities of the nose begin to tingle slightly. The result: a liar has an irrepressible need to touch his nose. Hirsch and Wolf analyzed Bill Clinton's statement in the Monica Lewinsky impeachment case before the Grand Jury. They noticed that Bill Clinton seldom touched his nose when he told the truth. But when he lied, he touched it as many as 26 times. Watch out with lying: you'll be found out sooner than you feared. ∎

IT WILL BE USED AGAINST YOU

Avoid making mistakes, however trivial they may be. And never mention facts that you can't prove. Princess Margarita de Bourbon de Parma said that she was being bugged during a chat with her aunt, former Queen Beatrix of the Netherlands. She had seen a microphone in the room. A fact that she could not prove. The Dutch security services immediately invited a couple of photographers to take pictures of a screw-head that the princess had mistaken for a microphone. We will never know who was right. But we do know that the princess lost her credibility in the incident.

YOU'LL LAUGH ABOUT IT, AFTERWARDS

A conflict often involves passionate emotions. And emotions make everything bigger and more intense. One question that I ask my clients in the aftermath of a conflict is: "Did it turn out all right?" The answer is always "yes". When you're in the middle of the storm of a conflict, it always seems more serious than it is. Try to be conscious of this during the conflict. It will give you serenity.

FURTHER READING

Arden, P.   *It's Not How Good You Are, It's How Good You Want To Be* (2003)
                             Phaidon Press Limited

Botton, A. de,   *Status Anxiety* (2004)
                             Hamish Hamilton / Penguin

Collins, J.   *Good to Great: Why Some Companies Make the Leap... and Others Don't* (2001)
                             William Collins

Covey, S.R.   *The 7 Habits of Highly Effective People* (1989)
                             Simon & Schuster

Fisher, R. and Ury, W.   *Getting To Yes: Negotiating Agreement Without Giving In* (1981)
                             Houghton Mifflin Company

Fisher, R. and Shapiro, D.   *Beyond Reason: Using Emotions As You Negotiate* (2005)
                             Viking Penguin

Gladwell, M.   *Blink: The Power of Thinking Without Thinking* (2005)
                             Back Bay Books / Little, Brown and Company

Glasl, F.   *Help! Conflicten. (2001)* (not available in English)
                             Christofoor

Pease, A. and Pease, B.   *The Definitive Book of Body Language: How to Read Others' Attitudes by Their
                             Gestures* (2005)
                             Bantam

Schelling, T.C.   *The Strategy of Conflict* (1960)
                             Harvard University Press

Sun Tzu   *The Art of War* (2003)
                             Penguin Books

Vergouw, G.   *De laatste minuut: de 7 mythen van het Duitse voetbal* (2006)
                             (not available in English)
                             BZZToH

Vries, P.R.   *De ontvoering van Alfred Heineken* (1987) (not available in English)
                             De Fontein

ILLUSTRATIONS

Thanks to: ■ Hans Aarsman ■ Deck Vormgeving ■ Ralph Edelstein ■ Martijn Engelbregt ■ Galerie Wouter van Leeuwen ■ Hotel De Goudfazant ■ Ron Galella ■ Gagosian Gallery ■ Peter Heykamp en Joep Luycx ■ Raymond Joval ■ Matthijs Kaaks ■ Jocelyn de Kwant ■ Rick Lightstone ■ Machine ■ Joep van der Made ■ Niels 'Shoe' Meulman ■ Parra ■ Ronald Reagan Presidential Library Foundation ■ Stephanie Rammeloo ■ Jan Rijkenberg and Joost Perik ■ Paramount Pictures ■ Spaarnestad Photo, ANP, AFP and AP ■ Nick Strong ■ Studio The Girls ■ Josie Sykes ■ Mirjam van der Vorst ■ Rudolf van Wezel.

ALSO AVAILABLE:

THINK LIKE A MANAGER
DON'T ACT LIKE ONE